WEALTH

PREPARE YOUR CHILDREN TO MAKE FORTUNES

WEALTH

PREPARE YOUR CHILDREN TO MAKE FORTUNES

How Parents Can Help Promote Financial Success in Their Children

IDA SUBARAN

Published by Best Seller Publishing®, St. Augustine, FL
Best Seller Publishing® is a registered trademark.
Printed in the United States of America.

ISBN: 978-1-966395-63-8

For more information, please write:
Best Seller Publishing®
1775 US-1 #1070
St. Augustine, FL 32084
or call 1 (626) 765-9750

Visit us online at: www.BestSellerPublishing.org

This book is dedicated with love
to Gita Héléna, Catherine, Gabriella,
Tiffany, Jordan, Jonah and Jonathan,
with admiration for the progress they
are making in learning about money,
while having fun doing so.

Advanced Praise

Ida Subaran's thought-provoking book targets parents and teachers of children from the early years to young adulthood world-wide. It offers practical suggestions on how to develop money management awareness and promote financial responsibility from an early age. This book is welcomed and is highly recommended to persons and entities charged with preparing children for successful adult lives.

– Georgia Bernard, Educator, International Expert, Parent Brussels Belgium

Ida SUBARAN exposes an important problem that unfortunately is widely overlooked.

Her many years of professional experience in the field of international education make her well qualified to tackle the question, and her country-specific examples should make parents attentive to the subject, and governments question their own provision of projects to raise financial awareness of the young.

– Edward A. Fisher, Chief Technical Adviser, GAMMA INSTITUTE, Paris, France

Contents

INTRODUCTION

This book is written mainly for parents, future parents, young adults, and those concerned about children. Its purpose is to promote awareness of the various facets of money management and acquisition, particularly those rarely recognized or considered. It is intended to help you assist children in developing the right attitudes, skills, knowledge, and experiences relating to money from early childhood onward. For it is widely known that:

- The early years, up to about ages 6–8, are critical to the formation of attitudes and habits that last throughout a child's life. Negative ones may be difficult to change in later years.
- During the early years, foundations are laid that are essential for further learning, skill development, and knowledge acquisition (e.g., mathematics).
- It is important to make the most of the early years by offering proper instruction—without forcing it—in order to help children develop positive attitudes, personality, creativity, curiosity, and aptitude.

Many children and adults in both developing and developed countries are poor; some are exceptionally poor. Some people may be poor because, in addition to having no money, they lack the skills or education that would enable them to work and earn money. In some cases, employment is simply not available. Other people are born into very poor families who suffer from a lack of basic human survival needs. These basic needs are unmet: there is not enough food (or a lack of a healthy variety of food), inappropriate or no shelter, insufficient clothing, and no access to clean water. They may also lack proper sanitation and access to health clinics and medicines. Furthermore, there may be no access to schools, no electricity, no roads, and so on. Other contributing factors in the context of their birth may include unfavorable political and governmental issues, natural disasters such as droughts, famines, hurricanes, and tsunamis, and other factors over which they have no control. Even those who earn a lot of money can find themselves heading toward destitution if their spending exceeds their income. The result of such living may lead people to employ desperate measures to gain money for survival.

The key to financial security is having money to afford basic needs, which sometimes requires setting aside money for inevitable and unforeseeable emergencies. It is obvious that one must have money before one can save money. If circumstances could be made favorable, people would be in a better position to achieve financial stability. It is, therefore, beneficial to learn to save and manage money wisely.

This book will guide you in teaching your children financially sound practices to avoid a life of deprivation and hardship. You will help them understand and appreciate the value of money and offer them a head start in all that affects them financially.

It is true that, in order to be truly successful, parents need to gauge their children's interests and abilities. Children may reject the idea because they do not want restrictions or discipline, and so parents may postpone the idea for later. Parents may also think their children are too young to understand or, because they have no income, that the subject of money is irrelevant to them. Such thinking is understandable. However, when children understand why it is important to be financially responsible, saving money becomes an interesting challenge or even a kind of game.

This book will help you, as parents, to see and accept the positive benefits of financial education for the young and your important role in this endeavor. The goal of educating children about money at a young age is that, as they grow and experience life, they will be spared anguish, financial disaster, or lost opportunities to better their financial success.

Parents, teachers, guardians, and other adults can all work together to increase awareness, knowledge, and skills concerning money, regardless of country or socioeconomic status. Rich and poor exist in all countries, but with proper education, we can teach our children to close the gap between rich and poor and to obtain financial security and success for themselves and their children.

This book is not a technical guide; it is based on knowledge of children, common sense, and exposure to children and families all over the world. One objective of this book is to raise awareness of similar experiences concerning money in countries other than one's own, to understand the impact of those experiences, and to work to improve them.

It is not the writer's purpose to recommend any banks, financial companies, or advisors/ consultants for any reason whatsoever. Instead, the writer's aim is to help readers develop a better understanding of financial issues, which, in turn, will ideally lead to better knowledge and wiser actions regarding children and money. With help and guidance, children can learn to value money and accept that saving, in a variety of ways, is not only essential to a comfortable and secure lifestyle but also can be fun, enjoyable, and creative.

CHAPTER 1

Parents – The Child's First and Most Important Educators

It is important to start early in educating your child about money. What he or she learns will be the foundation for future actions. You are the child's first and most important educator.

Parents

Parents are instrumental in the development of a child's behavior and adjustment, whether negative or positive. Therefore, as a parent, you should rightly accept as your responsibility the education of your child regarding money. This may not be as simple as it sounds; there are many factors to consider before you can present your children with an educated and effective system for balancing their budgets.

It is important for you to reflect on your own attitudes and actions, as you yourself may not have had any notions or guidance from your own parents. What have you learned about saving and spending? How are the financial aspects of your household currently run? It is perhaps most important to consider that while your child learns from various information sources—television, books, magazines, friends, the internet—they learn first and foremost in early childhood by watching you. By observing your behavior with money, by listening to you, by absorbing your discussions with other adults about money, and by observing your spending habits, children form a basis of understanding regarding their own handling of money. This informal education is very potent. They also learn from other members of the family, including siblings, so it's important to have a unified system that everyone in the household understands, accepts, and follows.

It is important to develop as strong an understanding of financial responsibility as possible from trusted and reliable sources before embarking on sharing that knowledge with your children. But before discussing how to obtain that knowledge, let's look at some patterns of behavior that work against your financial goals.

The Following Are a Few Examples of Negative Behavior of Some Parents Regarding Money:

- Overspending
- Buying unnecessary things
- Having no budget plan in place
- Having no savings plan in place
- Throwing away things because you don't like them anymore, then making new purchases that may be discarded too
- Arguing about money in front of a child

Parents are often bombarded with demands from their children for the latest jeans, another DVD, a mobile phone, the clothes their friends have, a toy they saw on television, etc. Many parents, if they can afford it, often give in to these demands because:

- Parents want peace
- Parents don't want to deprive their children—they don't want their children to feel left out as the only one without the desired possessions
- Parents love their children, and by giving them what they want, they feel they are expressing that love
- Parents may feel guilty for not spending enough time with their children
- Other reasons

It is important to remember one thing: **you are in charge.** You may feel inadequate in your role as a parent, especially if you really can't afford all the things your child asks for, but be assured, you are not alone. Many other parents feel the same way as you do and feel the same pressure to give in to their children's material wants. It's important to remember that you are not a bad parent because sometimes you have to say no. There are numerous lessons to be learned from that simple decision alone.

Also, there is nothing wrong with asking other parents or other adults, such as your banker or tax advisor, for tips and advice. You don't need to be a financial wizard or expert, but you must seek knowledge and use your common sense and creativity in the best interest of your child. Equipped with a sound base of knowledge regarding effective and responsible money practices, you will be better prepared to teach your child and respond to his or her questions.

You will discover many opportunities in everyday life to offer financial lessons to your child, from the supermarket to the bank to simply clipping coupons together at the kitchen table. These are opportunities to have fun together and strengthen your relationship. The realities of today's world guarantee that your concern as a parent never ends, and because you love your children, you want to do your utmost to protect them from struggling with money and spiraling into financial disaster, both as young people and as adults. This attitude is very laudable; however, it needs to be encouraged, promoted, and acted upon in meaningful and relevant ways.

Of course, this does not mean that you should overprotect your children. There is a difference between guiding them toward smart choices and working your knuckles to the bone to pay for their expenses forever or giving them all the money they need or request. Certainly, the latter is not the way to go! Instead, parents should teach, guide, and assist children while they are young to learn and develop positive money habits, along with the management and responsibilities that go with them, so that when children grow up, they will experience financial freedom.

Parents Need to Recognize Some Important Notions About Children!

1. Children are eager learners. They are curious and ask unlimited questions until they receive an answer they can under-

stand and accept. Parents should encourage this, as it is how learning takes place.

2. Children like money—to possess and to spend. You have likely observed this repeatedly; children will spend as much as possible if given the chance. Children receive money as gifts from family and friends at birth, on birthdays, or on other special occasions. They need to be taught that money should always be appreciated. It is an ideal gift, but it is not an entitlement, nor is there an endless supply.
3. Children, at a certain age, receive pocket money. They look forward to their allowance and usually try to negotiate an increase sooner or later. Be prepared. It is important to teach them that with more money comes greater responsibility. They shouldn't get into the habit of believing they can have something for nothing.
4. Children can be rewarded with money for doing tasks such as running errands or small jobs. They love this kind of reward! Plus, it teaches them that in order to earn

money, they need to do something for it—it won't just be handed to them. That makes money more valuable and spending more intentional. However, not all "jobs" should come with financial compensation.

5. Children are sometimes rewarded with money for success in school, sports, or other activities. Money can be a powerful incentive, but children should also understand that they can succeed without being "paid" for it. Achievements should be celebrated for their intrinsic value, not just for financial gain.
6. Children sometimes receive money from visiting relatives. Even if they don't immediately express gratitude—perhaps out of shyness or unfamiliarity with the visitor—they still appreciate these gestures. Parents should encourage them to acknowledge such gifts and understand that they are acts of kindness, not expectations.
7. Children take on odd jobs, get summer jobs, or create their own income streams. Encouraging children to be enterprising

boosts their self-esteem, builds confidence, and provides valuable financial lessons.

8 Children have the advantage of time in building wealth. A normal lifespan provides many opportunities to build financial security and develop financial knowledge, responsibility, and money management skills. It is essential to start early, instilling good habits that will serve them throughout their lives.

By teaching children responsible money management early, parents provide them with the foundation for financial success and independence.

CHAPTER 2

Help Your Child Avoid Money Difficulties

With the varied and unlimited opportunities in existence everywhere, you can help your child master appropriate skills and build upon individual knowledge, interests, and capabilities when learning about money. You should provide first-hand, concrete experiences for your child to learn what worked and what didn't for you. You're also encouraging your child to engage in critical thinking; he or she is absorbing facts, forming concepts, and using those to think soundly, understand clearly, and act with confidence and responsibility in keeping with that child's individual stage of development.

Keep in mind that children of the same chronological age are not necessarily at the same developmental age. Thus, you need to accept each child as an individual, as well as recognize his or her differences, and teach the child to work to his or her strengths.

Some Building Blocks

Every experience at each level will serve as a resource for the foundation of subsequent levels of learning. Some age-appropriate suggestions for helping to build that foundation are outlined as follows:

Age 3–5 (approximately)

At appropriate times and in relevant contexts:

- Talk about money with your child.

- Help him or her identify individual coins and their value, as well as paper money/bills, using fake and/or real money, depending on the individual child.
- Empty your purse or pocket and ask the child to count the coins; offer help as needed. Remember that younger children may be able to count correctly but may not understand what the numbers represent due to their developmental age.
- Play shop with the child using toy materials, where toys are bought and sold.
- When shopping together, ask the child to observe the prices of some items he or she plays within their shop; they can "sell" the items at home for similar prices.
- Give the child some money when shopping together to buy something they want. Ask if the money is enough, not enough, just right, or too much.

Age 5/6 to 10/11 (approximately)

Relevant to learning about money and in keeping with their age, individual differences, and experiences, children in this age range:

- Can count and understand what the numbers represent.
- Can understand comparatives (such as more/less, same/different, smaller/bigger, quarter/half/three-quarters/whole, some/all, enough/not enough).
- Can identify money (e.g., cents, dollars; centimes, euros; pence, pounds) depending on the money used in different countries, as well as their comparative value.
- Can add, subtract, divide, and multiply.
- Know that numbers represent something real.

Some methods you can try with children in this age range include:

- Offering an allowance or pocket money to learn first-hand money management.

- Starting around age 5–6 years, give half the amount twice a week and once a week for older children. Like yourself or other adults, children will look forward with great anticipation to receiving their allowance on a specific date—"payday."
- Guiding the child in planning how to use their money by setting easy and achievable targets.
- Not attaching strings to the allowance.
- Not punishing a child by withholding the allowance to express disapproval of something they did. Withholding the allowance for a long time may cause the child to resent you or develop subconscious stress about money in general (e.g., worrying that failure will result in never having enough). Some children may react by considering stealing.
- Explaining in simple language the importance of saving.
- Offering three piggy banks or other appropriate containers for money. Explain that one is for saving, one is for spending, and

the third is for "generosity." Explain the differences. *Note: This will be explained in the next chapter for reference.*

- *Making each learning experience attractive and enjoyable for the child.*
- *Not offering money as a reward for doing homework, which is a discipline contributing to learning and success, or for taking a bath or brushing their teeth, as these should be learned as a matter of personal health, hygiene, and respect for their bodies.*
- *Not giving a child money every time they request it; instead, teaching them that money must be earned.*
- *Praising the child as progress is made and encouraging further learning.*
- Helping your child understand that if they save X amount for a certain period, they will have enough to buy something they really want. However, this may mean they cannot afford something else. The child will need to choose. You should not control their decision but allow them to learn from the consequences. These decisions

may help children realize that immediate gratification is not always the best choice and that sometimes foregoing something they want now to save for something bigger or more important will be worthwhile.

- Helping your child understand the difference between "want" and "need" in the context of spending money.
- Helping your child make decisions about spending their money.
- Not insisting that the child save all the time or at any time from their pocket money. Sometimes, the joy of spending serves as an incentive to save. Use your understanding of the individual child.

Age 11/12 to 18 (approximately)

When working with children in this age group, you can:

- Recognize teens' changing spending patterns and discuss the reasons for the changes. Help them evaluate whether those changes are worthwhile.

- Guide and encourage children to find extra ways of earning money.
- Teach children to compare prices before buying.
- Avoid giving more money when children overspend, as this will help them learn through experience the importance of setting limits on spending and making relevant choices.
- Raise the topic of credit cards. If you decide to allow your older child to have one, it is very important to explain its purpose, how and when to use it intelligently, and the consequences of misuse, as well as the convenience. Work with them to set limits for use and establish a realistic plan for paying off the monthly balance. Always be available to answer questions and explain concepts repeatedly to clarify anything they need help understanding. You can help your child make appropriate decisions as needed.
- Teach children to plan ahead for money-spending occasions. If you are saving

for something special, such as a family holiday or vacation, share your plans with your children and suggest that they also save toward the event.

- Introduce and discuss foreign currency with children before they visit a new country.
- Other.

CHAPTER 3

Promote Financial Success

Savings

Children can learn to save. You can help them start laying the foundations for their future financial security and prosperity now. By simple arithmetic, he or she will have more money the longer the period of time for saving. Time is in their favor. But first, you need to explain:

- why it is necessary to save money;
- what they are saving for;

- how to set an appropriate target/amount to save regularly;
- when and how long it is needed to achieve their goal, as well as the rewards and benefits.

You may argue that the amounts earmarked for saving may not add up to much and that children, being children, should be left to enjoy their gifts and rewards. It isn't practical or effective to insist they save everything all the time or to set goals that are simply unreachable by children. However, with your help and guidance, your child can start to save a certain but realistic percentage of his or her money—bearing in mind the long-term goals. Let them know that they will accrue monthly or yearly interest on savings. In other words, financial institutions will essentially give them an additional (albeit small) percentage of free money just for banking what they earn, making them richer, provided that none of it is spent.

By discussing with your child what earned money can and should be used for, he or she can understand how far a portion of their total amount stretches and can allocate funds according to reasoned wants and needs. Referring to an idea introduced earlier to encourage children to learn about money, they can use the same containers or get other ones for this purpose.

Give your child three piggy banks or other containers. These could be plastic containers, shoeboxes, keepsake boxes, etc. Children should be encouraged to keep all of their money in a safe, secure place they will remember (on top of a dresser, for example). One container can be used for saving only—their "Saving Account." The second one can be used to keep money for spending—their "Current Account" or "Spending Account." The third one should be marked "Generosity." Explain that the "Saving" container will increase as more and more money is put into it, while the "Spending" container will change as spending takes place. In the "Generosity Account" container, some money can be saved to give to others in cash or kind. It can be donated to a cause, project, individual, or organization. This last account teaches children that recognizing the blessings they have goes hand in hand with recognizing the lack others may experience, and that reasonable generosity is repaid in many rewarding ways, far beyond the financial.

Encourage your child to put a certain percentage of his or her "income" regularly into the Saving container so it becomes a habit—a lifelong habit—while the rest can be put in the Spending and Generosity containers. You can teach them to add up expenses—their lunch money or the cost of going to dinner and a movie with friends—and to allocate at least that much into their Spending container. If an emergency arises, money may be borrowed from the savings piggy bank. However, borrowing, of course, has consequences; the amount borrowed must be repaid, and the sooner, the better. Teach them that while sometimes unavoidable, borrowing is not a habit to be encouraged or regularly practiced. Otherwise, habitual borrowing could lead to serious debt issues. It probably goes without saying that you should not borrow from your child's money.

From Piggy Bank to a Real Bank

Age 10/11 to 18 (approximately)

Although saving money in a piggy bank is an enjoyable way to begin learning about money and saving, children's savings need not be left in a piggy bank forever. As parents, you can suggest that the money be put into an interest-earning account. The fact that the money will gain more money (interest) in the bank, whereas it will not in just the piggy bank, will be a positive incentive. Furthermore, the temptation to spend frequently will be diminished since it is, in a sense, out of sight and out of mind. Later on, some of the money can be invested after seeking advice from banks, financial experts, or other adults with experience in this area and reviewing and discussing the various options available.

It is important to note that financial management should, at some stage, focus on goals, including saving for something specific in the future.

At this age, children are influenced most by their peers, the Internet, and the latest gadgets.

Therefore, they may try to negotiate an increase in their allowances before you even mention it. When this happens, be sure to remind them of "needs versus wants." You can also explain to them the concept of inflation and that in the working world, pay rates are usually only increased (aside from performance excellence) to keep up with the rising prices of goods and services. You may choose to increase their allowance as they get older or if they prove they can and will handle more responsibility.

Additionally, children can try to "earn" extra money by babysitting or finding new jobs around the house, school, neighborhood, or community. They will quickly learn that time management is an important factor in money management: If they don't make time for work, they won't get paid. If they spend too much time working, they will miss out on fun activities or items they want to buy. As a parent, it is important to help them reach a balance between working and playing.

Some may be talented enough to make things to sell, such as jewelry, greeting cards, artwork, or other crafts. This would be an important time to take stock of their talents, interests, and special abilities and to develop them even further.

The Bank

Now is a good time to visit your bank with your child if you have not yet done so. However, first, you should explain that the role of a bank is to keep people's money or valuable deposits safe, and so people secure their money there by opening one or more accounts. These people are called customers. The bank records the amount deposited in each account and manages any incoming or outgoing amounts to that account. It also monitors, to an extent and depending on the bank, the activity of the account to prevent identity theft and fraud. Customers can request or withdraw money from their account, and the bank will pay them that amount if they have enough to cover it in their account.

Another way of withdrawing money from an account is by writing a check for a specific amount using the checkbook that the bank gives each customer. The bank will then pay the amount in cash. The withdrawal will be made from a Current Account used for spending. Another type of account is called a Savings Account, used to save money. The bank will give some interest on the sum monthly or yearly. This interest is, in essence, a payment for the bank to be able to circulate your money through its facility. The benefit of interest is that savings will increase without the child necessarily having to do anything more to achieve it. The bank can also give financial advice and recommend services, which the banker can explain and recommend according to the needs of each customer.

The child will likely be familiar with a lot of this information, as he or she is used to saving. The concepts of borrowing, saving, spending, and making sure that there is never a deficit or negative balance in the account should be at least familiar to the child from their experiences with their containers.

At the bank, you can discuss with the banker and your child the best means for him or her to save (e.g., a savings account, bonds, stocks, IRAs, and other options). Be sure that your child understands and participates in the discussion in keeping with his or her abilities and that the saving method is legally appropriate for a minor or young adult. Explain to the child that he or she will have to put money—that is, a deposit—into any kind of spending account regularly in order to maintain a positive balance and should regularly deposit money into savings in order to increase available money for an end goal.

You may want to encourage the child by offering to make the first deposit into the account. Thereafter, the child should take over the task. To do so successfully, it is absolutely important to establish a plan to guide, teach, and encourage good money management.

Money Plan or Budget

A successful money plan or budget is dependent upon a few different factors. Income, for example, is an important and primary concern. Income for a child includes allowances, gifts, and payment for services or products offered by the child, among others. It is important for the child to see the comparison between how much he or she earns and how much he or she spends in order to appropriately decide how much to put into a current/spending or checking account and how much to put into a savings account.

It should be stressed to the child that money in the savings account should not be thought of as money that is accessible for spending—at least, not until a specific long-term goal is reached. As circumstances in the child's life change, so too may the percentage of allocations into each account.

To help your child understand more concretely the importance of keeping set amounts in each account, you can show him or her visually through a budget plan for a month. On a piece of paper or a computer, make a chart. The heading of the first column should be **IN/Income.** In this column, list pocket money, gifts, earnings, and the like. The second column should be titled **EX/Expenses.** In this column, include what is spent on items, events, and others, such as books, CDs, snacks, gifts for others, or some small amount given to someone in need.

If more is spent than what is in the account, then the child is said to be **in the red.** Explain to your child that being in the red means that now, he or she owes the bank money because, in essence, the child borrowed it from them to cover what was in excess of their account amount. That is when a realistic revision of the child's spending and saving plan is necessary. It is important to avoid this situation (i.e., having debt), as the child will have to repay the amount, often with interest, which can be a significant monetary loss for the child. After making a revised plan, ask the child to take note of the differences and the reasons for the outcome. This is a valid and important learning experience that will be useful throughout life.

On the other hand, if less is spent than what is in the account (profit), then everything is positive. This means the child is not only maintaining financially responsible habits but is also building wealth.

Harmonization of Savings and Spending

You will no doubt need to explain to the child that saving and spending have to be harmonized and that this is not always an easy task. Sometimes, it does involve one or even several re-evaluations and revisions of budget and spending/saving plans. However, with more and more experience, the child will eventually learn to master the task of making the adjustments needed. The child will realize that sometimes it is necessary to save more and/or spend less.

Assure the child that he or she is not the only one facing this problem—other adults and families, big corporations, international organizations, and even governments are also making a budget plan that serves as a guide on saving and spending money, and they often have to make revisions constantly as well.

When your child does fall into debt, it is not a wise idea for you to pay for the child's overspending. The child should be made to understand the consequences and responsibilities involved. This means that he or she will need to limit or eliminate some spending for as long as necessary to overcome the problem. No doubt, the sacrifice involved in making sure the debt is repaid will be a formidable learning experience. Lecturing the child may not be as effective! Be a good example for your child by staying out of debt.

At School

Teachers, like parents, may not pay enough attention to the topic of money in their interactions with children. However, they do know that the early years of a child's life lay the foundations for the forming of attitudes, learning, and development in all areas of his or her life. Still, this important knowledge is utilized mainly in areas related to schooling.

It is seldom mentioned or significantly taken into account that children also develop a positive or negative attitude toward money, learning to value it as well as understand its worth. Children learn the arithmetic of money but not the true value of it, nor are they often significantly instructed in how finances work in the adult world. Many assume that children will learn all that is essential when they become adults, but this may be wishful thinking, and by then, it may be too late to instill positive habits regarding money.

It is also fair to say that adults cannot pass on to children knowledge and skills they never acquired themselves. This leads to the perpetuation of otherwise avoidable potential poverty down a family line.

Schools, however, can offer a variety of different experiences regarding money. Children can learn in interesting, practical, enjoyable, and disciplined ways about the value of money, how to use it wisely, and how to set and achieve financial goals.

Furthermore, children will be elated to start their adult life with a lump sum—maybe a substantial one—instead of waking up startled by the need to save later on at the start of their working lives (the dilemma of too many adults!). Naturally, the amount in savings is directly related to the amount saved, the interest and dividends earned, and the length of time that this fruitful and thrilling adventure has been pursued.

It is beneficial to discuss with your child the types of life events that may arise and for which a healthy savings account will be a great advantage. Getting married, buying a house, buying a car, traveling to another country, and starting a business are all major life events that can require a substantial amount of saved money. It will be of great help to the child to have had money saved since childhood to help pay for these things.

Different Countries, Different Approaches

The following are some selected examples of formal education, government and non-governmental organizations, community efforts, as well as informal individual initiatives regarding learning about money and how to manage it for children in different contexts and countries. They highlight an enterprising spirit, school efforts, community collaboration, initiatives of young people, expressions of generosity, and a lot of creativity and imagination.

ENGLAND

At St. Ambrose Barlow Comprehensive School in Salford, school children learn "how to deal with debt, save for retirement, and even what constitutes ethical investment — all as part of the national curriculum." Previously, the school carried out a personal finance study pilot. According to the deputy head of the school: "Studying personal finance helps them with their mathematics and builds confidence." These children, aged 11 years and up, "have learned financial management skills and even run an in-school jewelry shop." Pupils under 14 years are given basic lessons about bank accounts and mortgages. Older pupils, 14 years and over, are taught about the possible implications of the financial decisions they make.

"The aim is to turn pupils into informed and critical users of financial services," says Mr. Steven Stillwell, the spokesman for the Financial Services Authority (FSA).

Involved in the program are the Department for Education and Skills (DFES) in consultation with the Personal Finance Education Group (PFEG). This group includes representatives from consumer groups, the City watchdog, the FSA, as well as High Street banks.

Parents also volunteer to give talks on money topics. [1]

SCOTLAND

The following is extracted from “Primary Step on Entrepreneur Ladder” [2]:

This example is a variation on the theme highlighted above, but it is very apt, as it illustrates that very young children can learn important money skills if motivated by adults. It highlights the development of the business enterprising spirit.

At Blackfriars Primary School in Glasgow, pupils as young as five are being given lessons in how to run their own company. At the age of six, they are already in business, making cakes and selling them to teachers and classmates for 20 pence. The children’s company, Star Bites, has already made a profit of £83.

Under a new scheme, which has been publicly funded and managed by the National Centre: Education for Work and Enterprise, the education staff was given one day of training in enterprise education. The accompanying teacher training pack helped provide them with the skills they needed to teach business studies to their class. One of the guidelines was that every enterprise project had to have customers. After some basic lessons, the class of six-year-olds gained valuable business skills. These skills could be added to the building blocks of reading, writing, and mathematics.

The Blackfriars head teacher dismisses claims that her pupils are too young to be learning how to make money. She believes that they are learning "necessary skills that could be put to good use in the future."

Tom Hunter, a self-made millionaire and former owner of the retail chain Sports Division, hopes the primary school initiative will create a more entrepreneurial culture in Scotland. He feels so confident in the scheme that he, along with other business people, helped to pay for its extension.

It is hoped that by encouraging these children to run their own enterprise at the earliest possible age, they will grow up with more positive attitudes toward business success.

NEPAL

A non-governmental organization (NGO) in Nepal, Child Workers in Nepal (CWIN), which is committed to advancing children's rights, started a bank for the many hundreds of street children working in Kathmandu, Nepal. These children earn money by doing things such as selling souvenirs, collecting money on public buses, and picking up discarded plastic. They live precarious lives on the streets, trying to hold on to their money, which may be taken away from them by older children. The children sometimes sew their money into the inside seams of their trousers or sleeves, and some simply sleep with their money in their mouths.

To overcome the problem of how to hold on to the money they earn, many children opened savings accounts with CWIN's savings scheme, which works like a bank. Customers receive interest on their savings, can withdraw money as they wish, and can also apply for a loan when they need one.

Rajan, a 14-year-old customer of the bank, says, "It has taught me the value of managing my money. I've learned that if I save, I can do a lot more things with that same money. Now I want to save enough so I can go back during the harvest festival and meet my parents."

The NGO believes that in the future, the bank will be able to offer help to many more children. "The money involved is small, but it's a fortune to children like Rajan and helps them to plan for a safer future." [3]

INDIA

With the support of the charity Butterflies, a group of Delhi's destitute street children started their own bank. The children themselves manage and run the bank, which not only keeps their money safe but also offers interest and loans. The bank has also given the customers hope and a chance to plan for their future.

A regular customer, 13-year-old Rajat, a rag picker, puts about 15 rupees (approximately 30 U.S. cents) of his earnings into his account per day. The bank has transformed his life. As he says: "Before the bank started, I kept any money I had in my pocket. It used to get stolen, or bullies took it from me. Now it is safe in the bank. Also, if I get ill and can't work, I can get money out of the bank and use it to buy food and medicine."

Another customer, Manoj, 12 years old, saves some of his earnings in his account. He is saving because he wants to start a small business one day. Afroz, 15 years old, took out a loan and became a trader, selling different goods from a hand cart. He paid back most of the loan with interest. His ambition is to save enough to run a regular shop.

Sebastian Mathew of Butterflies says: "The idea of savings is a new concept. So too is the idea that the money they earn is not just to survive; it can also give them a happier future." [4]

JAMAICA

Jane was a 12-year-old girl who lived in a rural district. She loved to recite poems and sing songs that she learned at school. She also attended church, where she learned other poems and songs, which she contributed to the Christmas concert. She performed so well that her reputation spread to other churches. Several churches asked her parents for permission for their daughter to participate in these additional church concerts. Jane and her parents accepted the invitations. She started attending the various rehearsals as her time permitted.

Jane also liked flowers, and she took notice of the vases filled with flowers in the various churches. One church used an empty tin as their vase. It was then that Jane began to think about how she could get enough money to buy a beautiful vase for this particular church.

One day, Jane invited her friends to play at her house, as she had something special to discuss with them. Her friends were so intrigued and curious that they all went to her house.

Jane then told them about the tin vase and that she wanted to give the church the gift of a beautiful vase. Her plan was to get the money needed by organizing a concert in her yard and inviting everyone to give a small contribution. Then she asked her friends for their help in making all the arrangements for this concert. All of them would volunteer to sing a song or recite a poem that they already knew.

Finally, the concert took place. Everything went exceedingly well, and enough contributions were made to buy a new vase. With permission, the group attended the church with the tin vase. Jane also asked her parents to accompany them. That Sunday morning, Jane made a very beautiful floral arrangement in the new vase and took it to the church. She and her friends waited until everyone was seated before entering the church. There, she presented the vase of flowers to the pastor, to the amazement and applause of everyone. To complete the gift, the group sang a song toward the end of the service.

This experience demonstrated creativity, generosity, and the spirit of sharing among young children.

PAKISTAN

A young boy used to accompany his father and his camel to the beach, where many tourists were sunning themselves or swimming in the sea. Father and son would lead the camel along the beach and pause frequently to invite the tourists to ride on the camel. They assured the tourists that they would lead the camel at a walk or gallop, so they should have no fear. Soon, some eager tourists took turns riding the camel—a new and fun experience. The tourists paid generously.

In addition, some, including the "not-so-brave" ones, wanted to take pictures of the camel, as well as of themselves with the camel. They, too, gave the father some money. When the father and son returned home, they counted the money and added it to what they already had.

This experience helped the son sharpen his counting skills, expand his knowledge of saving, and gain work experience. Later on, they planned to buy another camel and offer more rides, thus increasing their income!

PHILIPPINES

Pedro was only 9 years old when he embarked on a money-making project. On Saturdays, he accompanied his mother to the market, where she sold fruits and vegetables. He was very observant and helpful; he also liked being with his mother and learning from her. He noticed that customers always bought tomatoes, which he also liked because they were tasty and beautiful.

When Pedro was at home, he started collecting empty tins and other discarded utensils. He cleaned them and filled them with rich soil. Then, he sowed a few tomato seeds obtained from discarded overripe tomatoes and watered them regularly. He watched them every day to observe new plants growing from the seeds. Later, when the plants were big enough, Pedro placed the containers in different spots by the side of his home.

As time went by, the plants grew and bore delicious-looking tomatoes. Now, he, too, was able to sell them at the market. However, he kept some for the family to enjoy. His family, as well as the customers, congratulated him. Pedro was so proud and confident. As his sales and savings increased, he began to think of other mini-projects.

This shows how many limitations can be overcome—Pedro did not have a proper garden to grow his plants. He had interest, imagination, and initiative. He achieved success and was motivated to do more.

SAINT LUCIA

Keri had just finished high school successfully. She wanted very much to go to university, but she needed additional funds to cover all her expenses. Keri told her parents that she would find a job and save some money. This meant that she had to postpone going to university immediately. Due to the economic situation in her country, jobs were hard to find, and those that were available were low-paying. Nevertheless, she started out in a temporary job, but she was not satisfied. Her ambition was to study business, so she began to think about what she could do in this area.

Eventually, she quit going from one short-term job to another. She developed a plan and started doing something that she loved and was good at. She baked and decorated cupcakes from home. Keri advertised her cupcakes by word of mouth. Another step she took was to invite people to drop by her home for a taste. Thereafter, many requests for her cupcakes of assorted flavors were received for birthday parties and other occasions.

Her project was named **CUPCAKERY**. It became so successful that her mother and sister started to help her whenever possible, especially on weekends when they had more time.

Keri made enough money, in addition to a loan, to start her studies a year later. She did not abandon her project, as she recruited more help from other family members. Her project expanded even more, and now she makes exotic cakes! She hopes one day to perfect her skills in making beautiful and tasty wedding cakes!

FRANCE

Geraldine was recuperating at home after an illness. Her family provided her with books, CDs, and other things to entertain her and relieve her boredom. After using all of these, she asked her mother to buy her a kit of beads. She started to design bracelets and necklaces, a hobby that led to making colorful jewelry. She offered one or two pieces during her waking hours to friends who visited her. They were delighted! Eventually, others ordered some to give as presents for birthdays and other occasions.

Thus, a hobby became a paying activity. Geraldine's talent developed and became known. With the help of her parents, she saved some of her income, which continues to increase.

What is important about these preceding examples is that they demonstrate how creative, ingenious, and enterprising children can be, even at a young age. They are capable of grasping banking concepts, business concepts, and the value of saving versus spending. These examples reinforce the notion that early education in financial matters not only cultivates these positive attributes in children but also gives them enough self-confidence and pride in their work to seek even greater opportunities for expansion.

CHAPTER 4

CHILDREN GROW UP

By the time they are ready to start work, those children who have been saving money from a young age can plan to increase the amount they save. Their ongoing discipline will be cost-effective and rewarding as their financial demands inevitably and relentlessly increase.

Once they start working, these children should learn to budget their salary. For example, they need to determine what percentage to use for living expenses, pocket money, savings, entertainment, holidays, emergencies, charity, and even miscellaneous and unforeseeable things, depending on each individual situation. Ideally, savings should be first on the list.

Late Starters

Many children may not have benefited yet from the kinds of experiences and approaches cited in this book. Maybe they are about to start their money adventure. They may not know how, when, or what to do. Furthermore, they may lack the discipline needed. Even if children are late starters, that shouldn't discourage them from starting now to repair and/or plan for financial stability and success. Parents will need to encourage and explain, teach, and demonstrate. Unguided, they may launch into uncharted waters. Life's adventures can be fraught with many risks, including unforeseen ones. Thus, to be forewarned is to be forearmed, especially concerning hard-earned money. It must be emphasized from the very beginning that late starters should:

- be committed to discipline;
- master certain skills, such as money management;

- set goals with a detailed plan;
- take action as needed with guidance from parents as requested;
- never give up, even when discouraged!

How to Realize Your Dreams

The following is intended to alert and inform older children or concerned parents in need of guidance. However, there are many books, financial consultants, and experts available for more detailed and situation-specific consultation.

Realizing your dreams is not really different from achieving most other goals, whether related to work, business, studies, or special projects. The basic ingredients, besides the right timing and good luck, include imagination, goals, objectives and plans, discipline, and, of course, action.

Imagination

Everything we do starts with thought and imagination. We should start by giving free rein to those ideas. We need to be as creative as we are realistic and willing to take intelligent, calculated risks that do not exceed our level of tolerance or comfort. Excessive impulse or unnecessary haste should be evaluated. Imagination can find alternative solutions to obstacles or more efficient ways to achieve dreams.

Goals, Objectives, and Plans

This is the stage where we select and define our goals and objectives for reaching our dreams. The more specific and detailed we are about our goals, the easier it is to work toward achieving them. They should be refined and sorted into immediate, medium-term, and long-term goals and objectives. The objectives define how to achieve the goals. For example, a goal may be to own a house. The objectives identify specific ways or plans to find, buy, and manage the house.

Discipline

It is so easy to give up or postpone what we plan or need to do to attain our goals. But this is counterproductive and a waste of time. We absolutely need to persevere, with determination, in a disciplined manner to achieve what we set out to do. One way to stay on track is to keep visual reminders of our goals around—pictures of the kind of house we want to buy, the dress we want to lose enough weight to fit into or the trip we want to take. Visual reminders help renew our enthusiasm for our goal and strengthen our resolve to pursue it despite hardships.

Action

Action is needed to implement plans in order to achieve specific goals and objectives. A flexible approach is necessary, as changing circumstances may occur. Be prepared with backup plans, workarounds, and alternative solutions. Then, if emergencies occur, you won't be set back so far on your road to achieving your goals. But remember, nothing gets done without taking action. Without action, we will remain in dreamland or continue to dwell on wishful thinking. We should not waver. Only by resolutely persisting in our goals can we really succeed.

Looking Back: A Wise Father

This is the story of Sarah, a late starter who never saved until she started working, and her conversation with her father.

When Sarah started to work after graduating from university, she was very proud to receive her first paycheck at the end of the first month. She had already done some "research" and had plans for how to spend her money. She felt very pleased with herself when she finally bought and gift-wrapped presents for each member of her family. Thanks to her "research," everyone was happy because they got a surprise gift—one that they wanted. Sarah didn't buy anything for herself.

A few days later, she was sitting with her father, who asked her about her work, health, friends—everything he could think of. Sarah assured him that everything was going well. Then there was silence. Sarah looked at her father; he looked at her. And in a gentle way, he asked her, "Have you opened a savings account at the bank?"

"No," she replied, quite taken aback. "Only a current account." She paused. Hesitantly, she asked, "Why?"

Her father sympathized with her and explained that he knew how she felt about spending money, having just started to earn after years of restricted income during her student days. Then, her father taught her a great but simple and obvious lesson. Sarah was embarrassed that she had not thought of it herself. Her father told her how important it was to save some of her income every month—without exception, he emphasized, even if it was just a penny. It was a discipline, he explained, that would serve her throughout her life. How she wished that her father had told her that many years before! Sarah has never forgotten that conversation, and she has faithfully followed that lesson.

Some Suggestions

It can be argued that it is easy to theorize about achieving goals—both financial and those resulting from financial success—but concrete ideas are more helpful. This, of course, is true, but there is no blueprint for the achievement of dreams. Different things work for different people, just as different dreams and goals mean different things to different people. Still, we can benefit from some simple ideas.

First Things First

Children often see things in immediate terms. It can be difficult, especially for younger children, to see the big picture, and long-term goals may not seem immediately important to them. Sometimes, they lack the patience that maturity eventually offers. It's easy to find yourself guilty of spending money first and then thinking about saving any remaining funds after. A wiser way is to save from the beginning—to set aside a certain amount in savings and then create a monthly budget, considering the remaining percentage of money as your new total. When you receive your salary, you should, without fail, save a certain percentage every time. You can start with a low percentage and increase it whenever possible. You can also add any additional funds from your budget not spent that month to your savings. These ideas, if put into practice by you and proved effective, will then be taught by example to your children.

Often, teens might be tempted to spend carelessly, egged on by advertisements or shop windows or by trying to keep up with the neighbors, etc. But before doing so, you should teach them to ask themselves, "Do I really, really need it?" If an honest answer is in the affirmative, then ask, "Can I wait a few days, weeks, or months?" If the answer is yes, then wait. You may eventually forget or decide that you don't really want or need it anymore. However, caution needs to be exercised to avoid replacing the first desire with another without going through the same process. If you find you do need it, explore options for making the purchase as cost-effective as possible. Can you wait until it is on sale or on clearance? Can you find a coupon for a discount? Can you find another brand that is just as good but less expensive because it's not a brand name?

Does one store sell it for less than another? Try it! It's fun! You and your children can think of it as a challenge or a game that you are playing with yourselves. The results can be astonishing! You may find that you really need far less than you think.

Investments

Sometimes, investments are a popular way of trying to gain a lot of money to supplement one's income. Some lucky people live only off their gains from these investments. However, investments are most definitely not something to jump into blindly. You need to be thoroughly informed, selective, vigilant, aware, and not easily swayed by promises of millions. This is especially important for children to understand, as they are, generally speaking, more naive and more likely to be taken advantage of by unscrupulous people who know the children don't know any better. Banks and financial advisors can offer information and guidance. So can Certified Professional Accountants. They can give knowledgeable advice about different types of investments and combinations of investments likely to bring you or your child a maximum return sustained over a long period of time. They, however, cannot predict the outcome of investments with perfect accuracy. Serious advisors will suggest diversification of investments. The final decision will be the client's, bearing in mind that as that client, you or your child must learn how to manage risks as well as favorable opportunities.

Some superstitious people believe in investing in growing "money plants," such as the **Dieffenbachia** or the **four-leaf clover,** which they think will bring them good luck in becoming rich. People are free to do this, and maybe—just maybe—will be lucky. However, knowledge of investment markets and alternatives, along with a willingness to go with slow and steady methods for acquiring wealth, such as savings accounts, bonds, and retirement accounts, will do children—future adults—a lot of good and also give them a wealthy start in life.

As you will agree, our world is full of the unexpected—good and bad—as well as a multitude of uncertainties that cannot be planned for. Furthermore, a vast array of options and varieties of investments are widely available from which to choose. These factors cause parents to puzzle over what is best to do in the interest of their children. It is, therefore, of the utmost importance to be well-informed before making decisions on any investment. The following are some questions that may serve as guidelines. They are not exhaustive, however, and you may certainly think of others.

Some Questions to Ask

Goals:

- What exactly, as a parent, are my goals? Are they long, medium, or short-term?
- What do I want to make sure my child is prepared for?
- What would I like them to have in life that I can help them get a head start on saving for?

Options:

- What are the options available? How do I determine which ones are the most suitable for achieving my goals?
- Can I maximize my success if I choose a number of options to work together, or will that work against me?

Flexibility:

- Can my child have access to the money regularly or in case of need?
- Conversely, can I make sure the child cannot access the money saved for him/her until he/she is of a certain age or until a certain event takes place?
- What are the penalties for flexible access to that money?

Risk Factor:

- What level of risk can I take?
- How much can I afford to contribute to this cause?
- What are the possible risks of this choice over that one?

- How much risk is generally undertaken, and is that amount of risk worth it for the payout?

Inheritance:

- If I, as a parent, contribute to the funds to be invested for my child, how will it affect my inheritance and taxation status?
- How will it affect theirs?

Taxation and the Child:

- Will my child be required to pay tax on the returns of the investment?
- How much should my child reasonably expect to have to set aside for taxes in regard to this investment?

Changing the Type of Investments:

- As my child grows from pre-teen to teenager to young adult, is it advisable or possible to change the type of investments to ensure the best results to suit his/her needs?
- Is there a penalty for change?

- Will my child's portfolio take into account newly rising investments as technology, medicine, entertainment, and production change?

Guarantees:

- What are the real guarantees, conditions, and regulations?
- What can I be sure to receive in the best/worst of market changes and circumstances?

Charges:

- What are the charges, and are there additional hidden ones?

Which One(s):

- From the bewildering array of options from which to choose—such as savings accounts, bonds, cash unit trusts, investment trusts, societies, stocks/shares, trust funds, among others—how do I select?
- What will be best for my child's specific goals/needs/wants/future goals?

Scams:

- How do I identify and avoid scams?
- Who do I contact if I feel there is a danger I'm being scammed?
- Do I have any recourse for recouping losses due to scams?

Consultations:

- Who do I consult—banks, societies, companies, financial advisors, friends, other parents… some or all of them?
- Who should I avoid consulting?

As previously mentioned, you may have other questions. You may want to talk about the best options to save for college or whether government programs are available to offer grants, scholarships, and loans for specific groups or toward specific ends. You may want to know if one type of investment will work better for your real estate goals, while another is better for education goals. When discussing investment options, be prepared, know what you ultimately want to accomplish, and come to the appointment with any questions or concerns you have. Knowledge, in this case, really is power.

CHAPTER 5

INGENUITY AND CREATIVITY IN DEVELOPED AND DEVELOPING COUNTRIES

Human beings are fantastic. We have inner, untapped resources that can always be called upon to meet every situation. Everyone, rich or poor, has used some ingenuity and creativity to identify ways and means of gaining more money. People may be spurred by need, ambition, greed, challenges, generosity, or other stimuli. The results of human ingenuity have been both positive and negative, from great inventions and lucrative enterprises to theft and fraud. These initiatives (the legal ones) are as varied and interesting as the individuals themselves.

Illustrative of these initiatives are some examples of the use of ingenuity and creativity from around the world. This selection is only to provide information, not to prescribe any action on your part. They serve as an eye-opener into the lives of many and perhaps as inspiration to exercise your own creativity in achieving financial success.

Pooling

Friends, colleagues, relatives, business associates, students, or others form a group as big or as small as the participants wish. Within this group, people take turns offering financial support as a whole to help each individual realize a goal. They agree to certain pre-discussed rules for managing this system to ensure good results.

Each person contributes an agreed amount each week or month (or other set period), at the end of which one person receives the total amount to keep and use as he or she wishes. The accumulation then continues in rotation, with the recipient continuing to contribute like the others and a new recipient from the group taking his or her turn to receive the lump sum.

This system of investment or saving can be repeated or prolonged. If someone needs money urgently, that person may ask to have an early turn or borrow from someone in the group. Variations on the "theme" may be introduced with the agreement of all participants.

Animals

Sometimes, in developing countries, a parent, family member, friend, or another person gives a child a goat, calf, cow, pig, chicken, or some other animal. It is given with the expectation that the animal will reproduce and the offspring will be sold. In the case of a cow, some of the milk may be sold, or the chicken may lay eggs, which can be sold or hatched to increase the number of chickens. The child thus earns money, some of which can be saved, while some can be used to pay for the child's needs.

Jewelry

Instead of banking money, jewelry is bought—especially gold or precious/semi-precious stones—to be sold eventually at a profit or as part of a dowry. Some people feel safer owning jewelry, as they can move from place to place with it. In some countries, owning a lot of jewelry enhances a woman's marriage prospects, as she is considered wealthy, or her beauty is enhanced when she wears it.

Land

Many people in many countries value land greatly and, as soon as possible, will buy a lot of land or more. It may be used for cultivation, farming, building a house, gifting to an offspring, renting for commercial or residential purposes, or selling later at a profit to buy more land. Land and real estate are frequently cited as one of the most expensive ventures to start and one of the most lucrative when they pay off. They are often considered steady and standard methods of acquiring wealth.

Selling

Commerce is the heart and soul not just of economics but of nearly every facet of life worldwide. Anything can be sold if there is a buyer or a need. Selling may be done to earn extra money, as a supplement to another job, as a self-employment business, or as a major corporate venture. In some countries, women make sweets or cakes and sell them to children. Some make carved wooden figures or weave blankets and clothing for tourists. Some sell handmade crafts.

- A housewife who was the only one in her village to have a refrigerator sold ice cubes to others who were thirsty and wanted a cold drink.

- Some—usually boys or men—transport a block of ice wrapped up as carefully as possible to slow down melting and sell shaved ice topped with homemade fruit syrup. The greater the variety of syrups, the more popular and profitable the sales. In a hot climate, this is very much appreciated.

Raffles

Raffles are usually held when someone produces something they own—bought or made by a person. For example, a young lady may embroider or crochet a beautiful tablecloth to earn some money. She could sell it but prefers to raffle it because she believes she can make more money by selling tickets to as many people as possible.

On the day earmarked for the raffle, someone is asked to pick out a ticket from all the tickets sold, which are placed in a container and shuffled. This is done in front of all those present. The winner receives the tablecloth, and the young lady gets the cash to use as she wishes.

Rare Coins

Collecting rare coins may be a hobby or an investment. The collector buys rare coins from around the world, then keeps them until they can be sold at a profit. Sometimes, coin collections are inherited and can be auctioned off for competitive prices.

Antiques

Many lucky people inherit antiques. Others buy selected pieces from a flea market or elsewhere. The owners may use them at home with great care to preserve and protect them. Later on, they may sell them at a profit when a need arises. Others pass them on to their children as a legacy or an investment. Sometimes, a discerning and knowledgeable shopper can find highly valuable antiques sold for next to nothing at garage sales by those who don't know the piece's worth. The shopper can then resell their find for the true value of the piece.

Paintings

There are people who buy masterpieces by world-famous artists as investments, with the task of protecting them from theft or damage. Others buy from a selected new artist with the expectation that the artist will one day become famous. Thus, their possession will increase in value in proportion to the extent of the artist's rise in fame. As a discerning collector, you can obtain works of art that range from a moderate to a nearly priceless cash value—so much so that some paintings need to be insured. As an artist, you can offer your works for sale over the Internet, to galleries, at art shows, and to private collectors looking for the next brilliant work of art.

Sweepstakes/Lottery

Who has never bought a sweepstakes or lottery ticket with at least the hidden expectation of winning some easy money? We do this despite knowing the statistical odds against us winning! But someone has to win, and it could be us. Our luck may be in our stars! And as popular American lottery commercials suggest, if you don't ever play, you won't ever win. This is a money method to indulge in with wise moderation, though, as gambling can lead to even more severe money problems.

Stocks/Bonds/Insurance/Etc.

Sometimes people invest in the stock market. Many bank on the assured promise of good returns. Of course, there are many very rich people who earned their millions this way. Others attain a percentage of wealth. Still, others lose everything, including their capital. The outcome is as varied as the array of possibilities for investing in the stock market.

Investing in Children

You may think that this may not be exactly the kind of investment that is relevant to this publication. However, it leads to the question of money, and that is why it is included.

In some countries where there are no systems of social security, many families will continue to have children until a boy is born. From birth onward, this son becomes the center of attention in the lives of his parents and grandparents. The son will get more food than his sisters; he will be sent to school while his sisters remain at home to work, and so on. Why? Because this is the family's way of "investing" to provide for their old age. They believe that a son will care for them and provide for them, while daughters will one day marry and leave them for their husband's family.

Education

There are some countries where families will make enormous sacrifices in order to educate their sons as well as their daughters. They believe this will ensure that their children's lives will be improved, and they will earn more money. The children, therefore, will be better able to provide for and take care of their parents when they are old and without a source of income. Their educated children's lives will also be improved. The education of subsequent generations provides for the possibility of accumulated wealth passed from parents to children and grandchildren as well.

Investment Clubs

Investment clubs may be described as a more sophisticated version of "pooling." The main purpose of the club is to acquire more wealth through partnerships with others. It also provides the opportunity to socialize.

The group of people—not necessarily experts in investment—meet as often as needed to decide:

- how and where to pool money;
- to share interesting, challenging ideas;
- to learn from each other about the stock market and trading;
- to cut down on costs and spread the absorption of losses;
- to invest collectively and regularly in the stock market;
- to have fun in an informal setting like a member's house, a café, a pub, or a restaurant.

The club elects and appoints members with specific roles to run it and to act on behalf of the club to carry out transactions or other business.

Grains

In many developing countries, some people "invest/save" by buying or growing grains. They will stock them, use them for food later on, sell them to earn money, use them to grow more or exchange them with someone for something else, among other initiatives. They may not have money to save or invest, so the grains are a substitute that suits them and their way of life.

These are only a few examples given to illustrate how rich and poor adults try to increase their wealth. As can be seen, not every method listed above works for every type of demographic, nor does everyone always attain lasting success. However, there is likely to be at least one possible way—either listed previously or developed from your own creative and entrepreneurial initiatives—that has the potential to provide wealth if one has the right attitude and is disciplined enough to follow through.

CHAPTER 6

TAKE HEED

Childhood provides unlimited opportunities for creativity and exploration, including developing ideas for working towards financial security and increasing wealth. Children's minds are designed to learn and make fertile ground for planting financial knowledge, responsibility, pride, and management skills. It would be wasteful not to benefit from these early years. By starting early, you can help your children learn the value of money and to value the skills and talents they possess to earn that money. You will help them attain financial security and success throughout their lives by learning and mastering the necessary attitudes and skills.

As they mature, children will use money skills and habits to manage more effectively—with newly acquired knowledge and with appropriately widening experiences. They will be more confident in taking informed, calculated risks and making intelligent decisions with which they can live. Your children will avoid financial perils and lead more stress-free, comfortable lives in which they can enjoy their money. They may continue to receive increased gains based on their hard work and the steps they took to achieve success and be proud that wealth and success were not handed to them on a silver platter. They will be more likely to appreciate their success and not take it for granted or squander it. They will hopefully use some of their wealth to benefit those in need.

It is extremely important that you help your children clearly understand that money is not the only or the most important thing in life. They should be aware that while money can buy many things that contribute to everyone's well-being, comfort, and pleasure, it cannot buy happiness, genuine love, friendship, loyalty, or respect. It can provoke envy and jealousy. Money is an enhancement to life, not its sole purpose.

Do not encourage your children to aim to become millionaires overnight. Instead, help them enjoy each necessary step taken, one by one, in the journey towards their goal. There can be as much fulfillment in learning, understanding, achieving, discipline, taking action, and developing and mastering the different stages necessary for financial success as in achieving financial success itself.

Throughout history, small gains, fortunes, and everything in between have been made and lost, resulting in tears of joy or pain. This will happen time and time again. Hence, your child's financial security and peace of mind will depend on the choices and decisions made, avoided, or ignored. Their strengths, confidence, and vulnerabilities will constantly be challenged, but their perseverance will be rewarded, and their skills will no doubt be improved.

Teach them that they are in charge, always! They should recognize that there are no guarantees in life, but they should never stop looking for opportunities! They exist!

Bibliography

Internet Articles

1. BBC News World Edition. Knight, Julian. *Lessons in Money for School Children.* BBC News Online Personal Finance Reporter, 4 September 2002.
2. BBC News/Business. *Primary Step on the Entrepreneur Ladder.* 17 October 2000, pp. 1–2.

3. BBC World News (South Asia). Aryal, Menisha. *Bank Accounts for Nepal's Street Kids.* 27 June 2001, pp. 1–3.
4. BBC News, World Edition. McGivering, Jill. *Delhi Children Bank on Their Future.* 22 November 2002.
5. BBC News/The Markets. *Setting up an Investment Club.* 15 August 2001.
6. Indiana Department of Financial Institution Consumer Education. *Children and Money - Mini Lessons.* Copyright 1996, Dale Carnegie and Associates, Inc.
7. Garneau, Jess. *School's Out – Start Your Child's Financial Education This Summer.* Examiner.com, 26 October 2012.
8. Hodges, Kelly. *An Educated Allowance: Teaching Your Kids How to Save Money.* Seeitmarket.com, 26 October 2012.
9. Karen. *How Parents Can Help Their Children Manage Their Finances More Effectively.* Money.nuvo.com, 26 October 2012.
10. Luckerson, Victor. *Making Personal Finance Cool to Kids.* Business.time.com, 17 July 2012.

11. Office for Early Childhood Education and Care, Queensland Government. *Pocket Money*. March 2012.
12. Wall, Ginita. *What Our Parents Teach Us*. Wife.org, 15 October 2012.

Other References

1. Campbell, Hazel, and Campbell, Heather. *Pointers for Parents for UNESCO*. Kingston, Jamaica: Caribbean Images Ltd, 1991.
2. Hornby, A.S. *Oxford Advanced Learner's Dictionary of Current English*. Edited by Wehmeier, Sally. 6th ed., Oxford: Oxford University Press, 2000, p. 822.
3. Myers, Robert. *The Twelve Who Survive*. London: Routledge in Cooperation with UNESCO, 1992.
4. O'Brien, Karen (Senior Editor). *Children's Illustrated Encyclopedia*. 5th ed., London: Darling Kindersley Ltd., 2000, p. 440.
5. Piaget, Jean. *The Child's Conception of the World*. New York: Harcourt-Brace, 1929.

6. Rohwer Jr., William, Paul R. Amman, and Phebe Cramer. *Understanding Intellectual Development*. Hinsdale, Illinois: The Dryden Press, 1974, pp. 205–257.
7. Torkington, Kate, with Cassie Landers. *Enhancing the Skills of Early Childhood Trainers*. The Hague: Bernard Van Leer Foundation / UNESCO, 1995.

About the Author

Ida Subaran was born in Jamaica, of Indian descent. She was educated in Jamaica, the Indian subcontinent, and the United States of America. Ida has a Master of Education degree from Harvard University, Graduate School of Education (USA).

For many years she worked for a United Nations Technical Agency, as an international civil servant, in the area of education.

The author has lived in various cultural settings and has visited many countries in different continents. Her education, experience, and wide exposure have influenced and inspired the theme of this book.

Besides writing, she loves to paint exotic flowers and landscapes—some of which have been exhibited. Recently she published an e-book, for children aged 3+, in English and French, entitled ***The Date Palm Tree / Le Palmier Dattier.***

Ida Subaran lives in Paris, France.

Made in United States
Orlando, FL
07 November 2026

90339165R00062